Still Well In Wellwood

Larry Levy

BookLocker
Trenton, Georgia

Copyright © 2021 Larry Levy

ISBN: 978-1-64719-780-3

All rights reserved. No part of this publication may be reproduced, stored in a retrieval system, or transmitted in any form or by any means, electronic, mechanical, recording or otherwise, without the prior written permission of the author.

Published by BookLocker.com, Inc., Trenton, Georgia, U.S.A.

Printed on acid-free paper.

The characters and events in this book are fictitious. Any similarity to real persons, living or dead, is coincidental and not intended by the author.

Library of Congress Cataloging in Publication Data
Levy, Larry
Still Well In Wellwood by Larry Levy
Library of Congress Control Number: 2021916669

BookLocker.com, Inc.
2021

First Edition

Acknowledgments

Thanks to my father, mother, brother, and sister for their love And mostly for being my father, mother, brother, and sister. Without you guys there would have been no Wellwood for me.

Thanks to Grandma Levy, Grandma Pasarew, and Grandpa.

Thanks to Cat for her love and support and for the "Still."

Thanks to all those who read "When All Was Well in Wellwood."

Those who reached out to me. I truly appreciate the comments and feedback. You guys deserve bold and italicized:

Melvin Levy, Sondra Levy, Howard Levy, Joy Levy, Cat Levy, Dave Grauer, Fran Silber, Harry Silber, Helen Silber, Barbara Mendelsohn, Steven Pruce, Sally Pruce, Mitchell Kauffman, Vicki Kauffman, Paul Fribush, Jake Mayers, Estelle Levitas, Douglas LeviTAS, Wendy Levitas, Fred Kobb, Rosanne Fellerman, Billy Orlove, Wendy Thomas, Gail Goldberger, Laura Siegmeister, Mark Siegmeister, Randee Greenwald, Stacey Silvers, Jackie Silvers, Clarinda Harriss, Paul Levy, Daniel Levy, Rita Rosenfeld, Bob Heft, Steve Janofsky, Nora Meyer, JK Perdue, Beth Jordan, Loretta Clark, Emily Goren.

My favorite teachers at Pikesville Sr. – Mrs. Kinsey, Miss Fine, and Norm Froelich;
Pikesville Jr. – Miss Monaghan (It's Friday);
And at Wellwood – Mr. Nowack, Mrs. Goldberger, Mrs. Adelberg, and Miss Carroll.

I would like to thank every neighbor, parent, canine, and, friend of mine through the early years at Wellwood, Pikesville Jr., and Pikesville Sr. High.

Larry Levy

To my dear friends, Valerie Pet, Randy Siegmeister, and Gabe Silber. You left way too early but we still talk often. Thanks for all you gave me.

And to Angela and Richard Hoy, Todd Engel, Ali, Justin, Brian, And Book Locker for all their hard work.

To those
On paths divergent
May you find your way home.

Contents

Graduation 3
It's in the Bag 5
The Valiant 6
Rude Awakening 7
Sales 8
A Family of Funny 10
The Sting of a Lie 12
Harleys 14
J.C.C. 16
U.C.L.A. 18
A Serious Guy 19
I Looked Around… 21
It All Happens at the Library 22
Extra, Extra! 24
Gino's 26
Peabody, Continued 28
My First Stick 30
A Trip to Vince's 32
Mini Flick 33
Sidetracked 35
With My Tail Between My Legs 37
Record and Tape Collector 39
The 45 41
The Tape Wars 44
The House Painter 46

Frustration 101	48
Studio Art	49
The Cost of Freedom	51
First Beer	53
The White Bird	54
Unusual Cargo	55
Salmon Cakes	58
From a Trip to a Fall	62
A New Sound	65
The Band Without a Name	67
The Parties, Five	68
A Fair Weathered Friend	72
My Inspiration	74
One Way, San Diego	76
Jeans West	78
Milford Mill Swim Club	80
3501 Calvert Street	82
It's a Maryland Thing	83
The Civic Center	85
Attman's of Lombard Street	87
Put it Back	89
A Song to Remember	90
Epilogue	93
The Shed	94
About the Author	99
Other Books by the Author	100

(1974-1978)

Still Well In Wellwood

<u>Graduation</u>

Painter's Mill.
June 6th, 1974.

One by one, each student stood as their name was called.
And there I was in the spotlight; standing, waiting,
Passed over by my next three classmates.

My gleeful parents were huddled somewhere in the shadows
Not quite sure whether I would make it to the finish line.
"Oh God, what did he do now, and would you look at that hair!"

Was the master of ceremonies alphabetically challenged?
Or, was it a front office mishap after I submitted my form late?
All I thought about was whether I should sit back down,
Pretend no one saw me, and blend back into the darkness.

But then came my three seconds on the same stage
Where Goose Creek Symphony and Cheech and Chong
Entertained my friends and I the previous year.
So, all was forgotten.

And there we were, all four-hundred and then some,
Buzzing around in the parking lot after the ceremony.
"Goodbye, good luck, don't worry, I'll see you before you go."
Tears for some, relief for others, surreal for everyone.

II.

Some of my classmates went off to college
As far away as they could possibly go;
Farther than the basketball star
That out-threw me with a softball years before.

Larry Levy

An adventurous few took a year off and traveled cross-country --
Guys I had hung around with most of my life.
Others contemplated their future,
Held mundane jobs or worked for their dads.

For those of us that stayed behind, old habits persisted
But kicks lost their bluster.
Now there would be less wise-guys, characters, heads, jocks,
And girls to carry on with.

My gift to my parents was the purple cap and gown, the diploma,
And finishing something that I started back in second grade
When I first attended Wellwood Elementary.

But perhaps my greatest gift to them
Came in the form of hope and possibility:
The prospect of moving out of the house.

They did not get their wish but neither did I.
And just like a bad trip, I heard my father's words
Reverberating in my 17-year-old brain,
"High School is the best time of your life --
The only responsibility is to yourself!"

I had one foot in and one foot out.

Still Well In Wellwood

It's in the Bag

A few days after high school graduation,
And without any parental prodding or bribes,
I made the snap decision to cut off all my hair.

This rash action in no way meant I was conforming -- heaven forbid!
Nor did it imply a softening of my rebelliousness.
When school ended, something had been taken away from me,
From all of us I suppose, so it was just my way of reacting.

There were no deep philosophical reasons or promises to self –
I did what I really didn't want to do
Like going to sleepover camp or getting on a scary amusement ride.

I hid behind my forest of hair since Spring of my Freshman year.
I was used to the strange looks from passersby
Whenever I walked down the street.

But now I was in the aftermath of the protected years as a kid
And into the painful transition of becoming a man.
I felt a new phase of life about to begin
And like it or not, change was going to be the new norm.

And even if I were to become a weakened Samson
It would only be for a short time, the duration determined by me.
My hair would most certainly grow back along with my pride.

But just in case, and out of respect
For all that my curls and I had been through,
I saved my light brown clippings in a large yellow bag
And tucked them away in the bottom of my dresser drawer.

(P.S. 2021 – I still have them.)

Larry Levy

The Valiant

My godmother, who many years earlier
Had taken me on a magic carpet ride to Wildwood
Bequeathed to me her faithful chariot.

The 1963 Plymouth *Valiant* was a red, four-door sedan
That featured a push-button transmission
And the famous cast iron, slant-6 engine.
When I would sing the praises of the car to my dad,
He would remind me that Chrysler made tanks during World War II.

She gave me the car as a graduation present
Although neither she nor my parents referred to it as such.
I didn't care about the reason or the timing of the gift;
Her kindness and generosity were reward enough.

I adored the car from the first day until the last.
To my way of thinking, the *Valiant* was cool
So, I became a big fan of Dodge, Plymouth, and Chrysler.

On the way home from an afternoon swim at Pretty Boy Dam
My friend and I were cruising southbound on Falls Road
When I slammed on the brakes to stop from hitting a possum.

The guy behind me rammed into the back of the car.
My friend got out to survey the damage done to the critter
While I straightened out my bent license plate.
The other car was twisted from fender to fender.

My nickname growing up on Chokeberry was "Prince"
And my first car was a '*Valiant*.'

Just saying!

Rude Awakening

During junior and senior year of high school,
I made pipes, stash boxes, speaker cabinets, and a coffee table,
From the beautiful knotty pine, poplar, and mahogany
At our disposal in wood shop class.

I was stoked by the beauty of wood
And made many visits to Hobby Woods in Fells Point --
The home of purpleheart, bubinga, and African rosewood.

So, it was only natural that after graduation
I would look for a woodworking job in Fells Point
Right down the street from where I bought
My first piece of cherrywood a few months prior.

I began work at a furniture company
In a dimly lit warehouse with no windows
Where I stood all day and had a 30-minute lunch break.

For two weeks, and what seemed like an eternity,
I worked from nine-to-five sanding table legs
And then passing them on to the next station.

During lunch break I would walk over to Hobby Woods,
Talk to the guys on the inside who sold exotic wood,
And reminisce about the good 'ole days.

I was able to walk away from the job and not look back.
But the pragmatism of one of my father's favorite lines,
"Do you think anyone applauds me when I go to work,"
Stayed with me for longer than I wanted.

Larry Levy

Sales

After the harsh reality of working on an assembly line
Dashed any real hopes of becoming a cabinet maker,
I turned my attention toward other opportunities.

Sales jobs were plentiful so I took the path of least resistance.
Selling home improvements over the phone
Seemed like a quick and easy way to make money.

Every weekday night I would cold-call random people
And pressure them to buy siding, gutters, roofs, and fences
From a storefront on Reisterstown Road near the Plaza.

People would hang up, curse, or say "Yes" just to get me off the line.
A supervisor would walk around the room and offer extra dollars
To anyone that closed a deal in a time frame determined by him.

There were more subtractions than additions on my paycheck
Because most costumers reneged on their verbal agreements.
I lasted about two weeks with very little to show for it.

II.

My next attempt to carve out a niche in the business world
Came in the form of selling household items door-to-door;
Knives, forks, spoons, dishes, pots and pans, and glassware.

The company was located off I-95 in Laurel Maryland
About forty-five minutes from Wellwood.
First came the classes detailing the quality of the products,
Followed by the hardcore techniques of salesmanship.

Still Well In Wellwood

After one week of intense training, our crack team of specialists
Were transported by bus to neighborhoods outside of Laurel.
Our unstated mission was to convince women
They needed something they already had.

After one week of zero sales, I turned toward family for salvation.
I took my suitcase full of samples over my grandmother's house
And gave her the best presentation of my one-week career.

She listened respectfully as I cut a tomato with Samurai precision.
Then I tried to impress her with a catalog of beautiful glassware
But my grandfather thought everything was overpriced.

I knew I was in trouble when my family wouldn't buy anything.
So, I traded in my sales duds for a bathing suit and went swimming
With every intention of giving notice the next day.

I told my boss the job wasn't for me and walked out a free man.
But when I tried to start my car, the engine would not turn over.
It was 5 o'clock on Friday and I was a long way from home.

My dad had to come and pick me up in Laurel
And my car had to be towed back to Wellwood the next day.
In the end, the repairs cost me more than I made at the job.

Larry Levy

A Family of Funny

One of my best friends from Wellwood
Lived about two blocks from my house on Laurelwood Drive
And was one of the funniest guys I ever met.

In fact, his entire family got in on the act.
His mom was funny, his dad was funny,
Even his younger sister and brother who I rarely saw were funny.

When I was going through my pun phase in high school,
His mom would point at any object in the house
And I'd come up with an immediate play on words.

She was always quick with a joke, a great sport,
Nice as she could be and very pretty.
I credit her with my early love of language.

My friend's dad sold used cars for a living and worked long hours.
Whenever I was around, he rarely spoke.
I assumed he used up his daily limit of adjectives on his customers.

My friend used to say of his dad,
"He'd drive around in the heat of summer with his windows up
Just so people would think he had air conditioning."

One day when his son and I were contemplating
What to do with our lives, he turned and said to me,
"Listen, if you don't know what to do with your life,
Just go into business for yourself."

It was a brilliant revelation: a seed planted for future harvest.
But I was only seventeen and too young to appreciate his wisdom.
Plus, I had neither the funds nor the wherewithal to go rogue.

Still Well In Wellwood

My friend and I were something of an amateur comedy team.
He would say something absurd with a flat affect
And I would play the straight man and validate his claim.

During senior year, he and I were in the same English class.
We were studying Shakespeare's Macbeth at the time
And came up with the idea of acting out the famous scene
Where Macbeth kills Duncan.

He played Macbeth while the role of Lady Macbeth
Was bequeathed to me because, "I had the hair for it."
I was neither a lady in manner nor appearance,
So, when the time came for me to return the daggers,
It was decided that Macbeth should murder me as well.

Before he went away to college
Sometimes he and I would double date
If we were fortunate enough to find girls with a sense of humor.

His black, Oldsmobile Cutlass were the wheels of choice
Because he had the props at his fingertips; a fake phone,
A rubber chicken hanging from his rearview mirror,
And baseball cards in his glove box to give to the girls.

The fake phone was on display because he worked for the C.I.A.
The rubber chicken drew a variety of responses:
"I'm thinking about becoming a vegetarian,
Or, it's a reminder to stop and pick up a chicken for dinner."
A baseball card was given to every girl he met as his calling card.

I felt the loss when he moved out of the neighborhood
But I am forever grateful for his friendship and comedic influence.
I have since become friends with his younger sister who carries
The torch of wit, humor, and zest for life.

Larry Levy

The Sting of a Lie

In the summer of my seventeenth year,
My friend and I took a trip down to the Baltimore Block
To experience the underbelly of the city,
And the underbelly of women who removed their clothes for money.

The first place we entered was called The Stage Door.
It had a long runway that ran the length of the bar
Where the dancers would magically appear and start stripping.

The club was dark, smoky, and unlike anything we had seen before.
We were fresh out of high school
Where no one had bothered to teach us about the art of burlesque.

We stayed until we saw every girl dance at least once
Then walked down the street to The Pussycat Club
Because any bar with that kind of name deserved our attention.

Most of the dancers were our age or just a few years older,
And looked like some of the girls we left behind at Pikesville Sr.
We gave our eyes, ears, and olfactory cells a thorough workout
Before attending to our other teenage need – food.

We stopped at Harley's on Fall's Road off Cold Spring Lane
To feast on a hamburger sub with all the trimmings
Before retiring to a peaceful sleep and fantastical dreams.

I went back to The Block the next weekend, this time alone.
Once again, the Stage Door was my first stop.

The first dancer to take the stage was a redhead
That looked like Ginger from Gilligan's Island.
After she whittled her attire down to nothing,
I realized she was someone I needed to become more acquainted with.

I bought her a few drinks equal to a month's allowance
As we chatted about her career in nude entertainment.

"So, tall, dark, and obviously not eighteen,
What brings you down to The Block?"

"I'm in college for behavioral science
And I figured this was the perfect place to conduct my research."
Somewhere, my friend was smiling at this line.

After a few more drinks and untruthful conversation,
I asked if I could see her after she was finished work.

"Sure, she said, meet me across the street,
Right in front of the 2 O'clock Club.
I'll be waiting for you" she continued,
Whispering the last five words into my right ear.

So, there I was at 2 a.m. on East Baltimore Street,
Leaning up against a wall in yellow gym shorts
Waiting for 'my Ginger' to come to me where I would whisk her away
To my basement bedroom on Chokeberry Road.

It was the first I felt the sting of a lie.

Larry Levy

Harleys

Harleys was located on Falls Road
Just north of Cold Spring Lane and I-83
And across from Poly Western High School.

Harleys was one step up from Little Tavern Hamburgers
Which was one step up from Stewart Sandwiches
Where a burger sealed in a plastic bag
Came to life in an infrared oven.

The Falls Road location was carryout only
Which didn't stop my friend and I
From ordering whole hamburger subs with 'everything'
In the wee hours of the morning.

They served their hamburgers from a vat, with tongs.
Rule #1: if someone pulls your burger from a vat with tongs
You may want to consider another outlet for your appetite.

If the vat was empty, an associate would bring in another bin
From somewhere around the corner, meaning you never saw
Where the burgers began their life.

Which brings up rule number two:
If you don't know the origin of said burger
You may want to consider another outlet for your appetite.

I preferred my sub plain: just the burgers and roll.
My friend ordered his with all the jazz
And claimed he never slept better in his life.

We always ate our bounty in the front seat of his Oldsmobile.
It was difficult to navigate because the roll was dripping with juice
And my friend was a stickler for keeping his car spotless.

Still Well In Wellwood

We loved Harleys! It was good eatin'!
But I'm not sure if it was as much the food
As it was the thrill of staying up late and having a full meal
When the moms that normally fed us
And fed us *normally*, were fast asleep.

Happily, our teenage foodfest lasted only a few months.
My newly acquired habit of eating before bed
Began but did not end at Harleys.

J.C.C.

The Jewish Community Center on Park Heights Ave,
Also known as the J.C.C., or the 'J' to us regulars,
Was *the* place to work out, play basketball, swim,
And hang with friends during junior and senior high.

After graduation, I still took advantage of the facility
Because you couldn't beat the low membership rates.
It also had a decent cafeteria in the basement.

I had my first ever Pepsi Cola 'on tap' –
Hands up, the best fountain soda I ever tasted.
Their hamburgers were also very good.

I mostly used the small but well-equipped weight room
Because in my late teens and early twenties
I was into bulking-up my otherwise skinny frame.

I remember walking down the hallway after check-in at 'the cage'
And seeing old men getting twisted like pretzels
At the hands of these huge, muscular masseurs.

I imagined a completely different scenario.

Sometime in the future, with the door closed,
Two lovelies named Heidi and Ursula
Would work me over as they saw fit.
Ah, but I digress.

I also tried the sauna and steam room for the first time.
I preferred the sauna not because it replicated
The historical and current middle east environment of my people,
But as a sensualist there was no equal to how the heat felt on my skin.

Still Well In Wellwood

The steam room however was a hazy, lazy, crazy maze,
Where much to my discomfiture no one was visible.
Plus, there was a whole-lotta-loogie-hockin' going on.

But not everyone felt this way about purposely trying to sweat.
On the wall in the locker room was a contest sign-up sheet
For all those who wanted to test their endurance in the steam room.

I noticed that the reigning champ was the father of a guy
I went to Pikesville with who was a great basketball player
And an all-around nice guy.

His father owned a sporting goods store in Mondawmin Mall
And in his spare time trained for steam room competitions.
He was in great shape for the event and smoked a cigar to prove it.

It was the craziest thing I ever heard of –
A short, stocky bald man sitting buck naked with other naked men
In a cloud full of hot steam, smoking a stogie –
And emerging victorious!

I'm not sure what the prize was other than bragging rights,
But if the Olympics were progressive enough to add the sport
He could have been a contender.

Throughout the late 60's and mid 70's when I was a member,
The J.C.C. was a club dominated by guys, doing 'guy' things.
As one fellow 'J' man once said to me,
"If you want to see women, go work out at the 'Y'!"

Larry Levy

U.C.L.A.

There was an alternative for us high school screw-offs
Who goofed around in class, cut school regularly,
And still wanted to go to college.

The answer was handed down to me on a backyard basketball court
From the leader of our neighborhood who phrased it thusly:
"If you do bad in high school, don't worry;
Just go to U.C.L.A for a year and then switch to a better school."

"But I thought U.C.L.A. was a real school," I asked in disbelief.
"Oh, not that U.C.L.A., the one here in Baltimore," he said.
"Where is there a U.C.L.A. campus here in Baltimore?" I asked.
"In Catonsville, The University of Catonsville Left of Arbutus,"
Or *Cate State* as most people call it," he said as he took a layup.

I went home that day very excited about going to college
Particularly if it meant staying at home, in the neighborhood.
Plus, the advice came from someone who would still be around
And knew how to offer guidance to underachievers like myself.

I reasoned that high school didn't really have to end,
A rationalization that quelled any fears about radical change
That would take me away from the friends and places I loved.
And after all, it would be just like going into the '13th grade'.

So, heeding my hoop-shooting, mentor's advice,
And knowing full well I had to do something,
I set my sights on U.C.L.A.

Still Well In Wellwood

A Serious Guy

Cate State was well-known for its pragmatic leanings,
Offering an array of two-year programs
From auto repair and nursing, to electronics and refrigeration – brrr!

But in the fall of 1974, I signed up for Math, Philosophy,
Creative Writing, and the required, Introduction to English.
Except for math my head spent most of the time in the clouds.

As I made the safe decision to stay at home,
Most of my friends were absorbed into the university system
That took them far and wide across the country.

So, I became a serious guy.
I took twelve credits and went to school three days a week.
When I wasn't in class, I spent my free time reading
And writing term papers.

In high school, I skated through most of my classes
And never gave much thought to any of my assignments.
Now I was so enamored with learning I created work for myself.

If one book or author led me to another, I went with it.
The same with writing.
I looked for ways to incorporate poetry into prose
And philosophy into all aspects of my life.

Every Saturday night instead of going out I stayed home
And watched the great line-up of comedy on T.V.:
*All in the Family, The Jefferson's, Mary Tyler Moore,
Bob Newhart,* and at 10pm, *The Carol Burnett Show.*

Larry Levy

The sitcoms I never thought about beyond the jokes and laughter
Were much more interesting now from an analytical perspective.
I even became serious about funny.

My father, who tried to live vicariously through me,
And clearly wanted me out of the house,
Reminded me that I should be, "living it up"
And that seventeen was the best age to, "get laid."

Having burned the candle at both ends during high school,
And coming off the breakup of my first girlfriend,
I had very little interest in the social scene at Catonsville.

And once philosophy got its hooks in me,
It was the only mistress I wanted to pursue.

I Looked Around…

…and they were gone.
My best friend from Northbrook -- off to North Carolina for school.
Another great friend from Maurleen Road set sail to see America
With a few other mugs I knew from school.

My gal pal from down the street ran with the ponies,
Her first and enduring love.
My hopscotch and Beatles' Second Album friend from Tamarac Court
Went away to school and I never saw her again.

Up the street in Chokeberry Court was no different.
The pretty girl I played spin-the-bottle with
And who accompanied me on Bar and Bat Mitzvah dates – gone.

The Doctor of Soul and Leslie West aficionado off to college.
Many other neighborhood kids who were less active on the scene
Flew under the radar and quietly disappeared.

The de facto leader of the neighborhood remained
But the realization that life on Chokeberry was rapidly changing
Left him with the blues on a grand scale.

He and I still hung out but it wasn't the same.
Gone were the carnivals to pick up girls,
Baseball across the street, and hanging out on his side porch.

I began seeing more and more of his next-door neighbor;
First on the down low and then more publicly,
But even that was sporadic as she was away at school.
The change was college and the natural slide into seriousness.

I looked around and they were gone.

Larry Levy

It All Happens at the Library

As I became more entrenched in my studies
I needed an immediate retreat where I had an abundance of references
And a quiet place with no distractions.

I soon discovered the 5th floor of the Cate State library.
As you ascended the stairs from the main level,
Each floor became smaller until you reached the top floor.

There were several aisles of books that contained what I needed,
Plus, a few small tables and chairs to stretch out and get comfortable.
It was the perfect place to study, doze off, and be left alone.

It was also the perfect place for couples to break from their studies,
And take anatomy and physiology to another level.
My top floor getaway became a scene, man!

Making out was one thing, I would have gone in for that myself.
But when the mile-high club invaded my space,
I knew I had to come up with an alternative plan.

So, I found a new spot outside the main entrance to the library.
There were cushy chairs where you could sit all day in comfort
Although there was considerably more foot traffic and commotion.

One day I was sitting next to a guy that was in one of my classes.
His cousin and I were best friends, and the three of us
Used to bowl ducks at the alleys in Greenspring Shopping Center.

He asked me if I had the notes for the English class he missed.
I flipped through my notebooks to try and help him out
When four knockout girls surrounded the chair where he was sitting.
One girl sat down on his lap and started playing with his shirt.
"You lost a button. I'll sew it on for you if you want?" she asked.

Still Well In Wellwood

"No, I'll do it – No way, I'll sew it on for him, No, let me."
Said the other three girls fighting over who would have the honor.

Nowhere in my English Lit or Philosophy books
Was there anything about how to deal with envy
Which I suppose was at the heart of my frustration.
So, it is probably best to end the thread of this story here.

Larry Levy

Extra, Extra!

Coincidence struck when I found a job listed in the *Evening Sun*
Looking for someone to deliver
The very same newspaper now in my possession.

There were only three prerequisites for the job:
Having a reliable car, a flexible daytime schedule,
And being able to throw things out the window while in motion.

I was good with all three, particularly the part about throwing.
The pay was $150 per week and I was hired on the spot.
I was an independent contractor, and the only time I saw my boss
Was on Friday when he handed me a check.

Every afternoon around 2pm
I picked up 300 copies of the *Evening Sun*
At Windy Valley, on the corner of Joppa and Falls Rd.

This fit in perfectly with my full-time course load at Cate State
Because all my classes were in the morning.
I was out of school by noon, and after lunch at Gino's,
I was off to start my route by 2pm.

The red *Valiant* was the perfect car for jockeying newspapers
In and around Northern Baltimore County
Because it had four doors and an enormous trunk.

I would pop a homemade cassette tape into the Teac
That sat in the metal glovebox on the metal dashboard
And groove loudly to my favorite music.

When I wasn't stuffing papers into a plastic tube
I was chucking bagged ones out the passenger's side window
While circumnavigating the wheel between my legs.

Still Well In Wellwood

One Saturday, I was loading the always heavy weekend news
From the steep loading dock at the State Police Department,
When the parking brake disengaged
Sending the *Valiant* into a concrete embankment.

I was able to get the car out of the ditch
And continue my route as normal,
But my four-wheeled friend was never the same.

Larry Levy

Gino's

When I finished my Monday, Wednesday, and Friday classes
I drove out of Cate State, turned left on Rolling Rd,
Then right on Frederick Rd and headed right to Gino's for lunch.

I was bone-skinny in those days so I could eat whatever I wanted.
On school days I feasted on two Gino *Giants*, fries, and a Coke
Before driving over to Windy Valley to begin my newspaper route.

My daily tab usually ran around five-bucks,
And the meal stayed with me until I got home from work.
The best part? It didn't ruin my dinner as predicted by my mom.

My brother, sister, and I grew up on Burger Chef's *Big Chef*
Which was a triple-breaded sandwich with two hamburgers,
American cheese, and a special sauce that looked and tasted
Like a mix of Russian dressing and relish.

We loved the *Big Chef* because it had no onions
As the three of us were not keen on the cry-baby vegetable.
The Gino *Giant* was also an excellent sandwich
And tasted very similar to the *Big Chef*.

But where it all began for me was back in the 60's
When my mom took me to Gino Marchetti's on Reisterstown Road,
Midway between Northern Parkway and the Plaza.

What Marchetti's had that the other chains did not was the drive-in.
My mom would pull up in her 60's Ford *Fairlane*, order from the car,
And then wait for the waitress to bring our food to us.

Still Well In Wellwood

At first, I just had a plain hamburger, but soon graduated to the *Giant*
Which paved the way for every 'super' sandwich thereafter.
If my brother, sister, and I had had our druthers,
We would have eaten burgers every night of the week.

After Gino Marchetti's closed, Burger Chef was our go-to place.
My mom took us there every Tuesday when my father worked late.
But all that would change when Burger King came to town.

Peabody, Continued

After high school and the somewhat subdued summer that followed,
I decided to continue my percussion studies at the Peabody Institute
While working part-time and taking a full course load at Cate State.

With the *Valiant*, I could drive to Peabody instead of taking the bus.
I still hung out in the small park that was between the school
And the beautiful Methodist church on the other side of the street.

I was progressing with jazz though my heart wasn't really in it.
I preferred classical drumming because I could apply
The hand techniques to the rock music I adored.

Theory classes were included in the tuition
And populated by eight, nine, and ten-year-old prodigies who
Made me feel out of place and ill-prepared.

I had trouble with melodic dictation and sight singing
Both of which involved hearing subtle fluctuations in pitch.
All my years of drumming did nothing to prepare me
For the onerous task of writing out lines of music
Played on piano by my teacher in front of the class.

I could not hear a note and tell the teacher what that note was.
But I heard melodies and harmonies in my head
And was able to write out music based on key signatures;
A mathematical approach that I could more easily relate to.

When Theory I ended, I began taking piano lessons.
I realized the fundamental importance of the instrument
And the obvious gap in my musical education.

I soon discovered the Peabody music library;
A stone's throw from the percussion room

Still Well In Wellwood

Also located in the basement of the Preparatory.
The library had a dozen Philips turntables, headphones,
And just about every classical record imaginable.

On Saturdays, after percussion ensemble,
I would sit in the music library for hours
Listening to the great composers.

My interest in classical music increased
But more importantly my understanding of melody and harmony.
I started to see music as architecture in motion
And the structure of compositions became easier to comprehend.

When I stopped taking formal drum lessons
I went back into the world of rock a much better player.
I was grateful for the thorough education received at Peabody
But now it was time to apply what I learned in my head
Without losing the feeling in my soul.

Larry Levy

My First Stick

After abusing my red *Valiant* for the purpose of earning a living,
And then carelessly letting her roll into a ditch,
I concluded that, "Man cannot live by one car alone."

With the money saved from serving newspapers
I began to look for a second car that would be fun to drive
And had the look and feel of a sports car.

The 60's British TV show, *The Avengers*,
Featured the sex-kitten, Diana Rigg as Emma Peel who was seen
Rolling down the English countryside in a cool Roadster.

In the 70's, England was still producing some great automobiles:
The Jaguar *XKE*, the *TR6* and *Stag* by Triumph, the *MGB*,
As well as other cars made by British Leyland.

I chose the affordable and miniscule, MG *Midget*.
For $2200 I snagged a two-year old 1973, maroon convertible
That looked more like a fancy go cart than a car.

Because this was my introduction to a manual transmission,
I called upon the experience of my VW *Beetle* driving father
To assist in my automotive education.

He drove me to the parking lot at Pikeville Senior High,
Explained the 'H-pattern' (which on the MG was very tight),
And taught me how to synchronize the clutch, gas, and gears.

For about one year the good outweighed the bad.
The car handled like a dream with its rack 'n pinion steering,
Making the twists and turns on Greenspring Valley a real blast.

Still Well In Wellwood

It was a convertible and that meant fun anytime, night or day.
I preferred nighttime top-down driving when the temps were down.
I'd find a side street to park, catch a buzz, and stare at the stars.
Sometimes I'd take a female companion and we'd stare at each other.

But like a bad girlfriend the MG always let me down.
I had to carry around a crowbar, to tap the starter
Whenever I was on level ground.
If that didn't work, I had to ask someone to push me
So, I could turn the engine over manually by popping the clutch.

One Friday afternoon at rush hour, I got stuck in first gear
Causing a major backup on the ramp at Charles Street and I-83.
Drivers gave me dirty looks, the finger,
And hurled obscenities at me I had never heard before.

I locked the car, walked over to University of Baltimore,
And called my dad who rescued me about an hour later.
The next day the *Midget* was back in our driveway.

I decided it was time to sell the car and move on.
My friend and neighbor who lived in Tamarac court
Loved the MG, warts, and all.

He gave me $1900 for the car.
He kick-started his way to school every morning
And kept it going for years.

Like our patriots and founding fathers
I extricated myself from the British
And looked to the colonies for my next set of wheels.

Larry Levy

A Trip to Vince's

There were two pizza joints vying for my attention
At the end of high school and the beginning of college,
That were separated by a few miles stretch on Reisterstown Road.

Louise's in the Fallstaff Shopping Center
Had both an eat-in restaurant and carryout
Each with their own separate entrance.

If I was on the run, I'd grab a sub, fries, and soda, and eat in my car.
When I took my girlfriend out for dinner,
We'd sit in the dining room and order Italian food from the menu.

The food was good for a local haunt
But not in the same league as the Italian food served in Little Italy.
Louise's carryout food was as good as most places around town.

Vince's also offered sit-down dining in a more casual environment.
There were about a dozen or so small tables and chairs
But no wait staff like Louise's had.

I preferred Vince's because it was more laidback and less hectic.
Plus, the subs were far superior to any I had had at the time.
They also played great music.

Among the locals, Vince's was thought to have had a brothel upstairs
Although no one knew for sure where the rumor came from.
I always suspected it was just an old husband's tale.

Regardless of what women may have been doing
Above our heads while we ate, the mere thought of such activity
Added a certain mystique and excitement to the place.

Mini Flick

I spent many a day going to the movies in and around Baltimore.
The Pikes, Crest, and Plaza were all located on Reisterstown Road
And were the three theaters my family, friends, and I went to the most.

The Pikes was where I saw *A Hard Day's Night*, *Help*,
And just about every James Bond and Clint Eastwood movie.
Plus, the Suburban House Restaurant was right next door.

The Plaza was cool because a movie turned into an afternoon event.
After a movie, my friends and I would hit all the stores in the mall,
Then walk to Hot Shoppes Jr. for a burger before calling it a day.
The Plaza theater was also the perfect place to enjoy a new girlfriend.

The Crest was hands down the largest and most beautiful of them all.
You could burn off the calories from all the candy consumed
Just by walking back and forth from the concession stand to your seat.
The Crest had a large balcony that gave the theater a touch of class.

My neighborhood friend who lived in Tamarac Court loved the Crest.
His mom would take he and I to see musicals like *Mary Poppins*
While his dad preferred the comedy of Laurel and Hardy.
An evening show meant staying up past our bedtime.

In the late 60's, my brother and I saw *Planet of the Apes*
At the Uptown theater on Park Heights Avenue.
After the show we went to Luskin's to check out the latest in stereo,
Then walked across the street for a Silber's chocolate cupcake.

In 1973, the Mini Flick theaters opened in the heart of Pikesville
And completely changed the entire movie experience.
It was a radical departure from the more utilitarian houses of old.

Larry Levy

The Mini Flick was home to two theaters: Mini Flick I, and 2
Each with about 150 seats in a very intimate setting.
The seats were *the* most comfortable my young *tuchus* ever occupied.

The sound system was also top shelf and loud.
Watching a movie was now like being in your living room --
Well, not our living room, because my parents kept my brother and I
From enjoying anything that involved their furniture.

Emmanuelle, a French erotic film, came out in the summer of 1974;
An X-rated movie popular with women in France
And most likely every red-blooded male on the planet.
The fact that the Mini Flick showed the film was radical for the time.

Fortunately, my friend and I saw things no one warned us about
Because if they had our fantasies would have been severely curtailed.
It was as if Playboy magazine had come to life on the screen.

I still went to other theaters depending on what was currently playing
But all things being equal I chose the Mini Flick every time.

Sidetracked

In the mid 70's my musical tastes began to widen
Thanks to several years of percussion studies at Peabody
And greater proficiency on the drum set.

I had been taking the bus down to Peabody during high school
But once the *Valiant* and I became compadres
The trips to the school and the city in general became more frequent.

One Saturday, I drove to Sherman's Book store on Mulberry Street
And found myself in the record bins for several hours;
Not an uncommon occurrence in those days.

I took a chance on *Hymn of the Seventh Galaxy*
The third recording by Chick Corea and Return to Forever.
It was my first exposure to what was then called 'Fusion.'

When I returned home and listened to my new record,
I did not understand what I heard – it was over my head.
But I kept listening every day for the next several weeks.

Lenny White's drumming was intricate and complex.
A mixture of funk, rock, and jazz, played at extremely fast clips
Appealed to my mathematical way of thinking about music.

In 1975, I went to see Chick Corea and Return to Forever
At Shriver Hall on the campus of Johns Hopkins University
And then shortly after at Painter's Mill theater.

I was learning jazz drumming from my instructor at Peabody,
And my brother's newfound interest in jazz guitaring
Began to find its way into my listening and playing as well.

Larry Levy

He was a fan of the jazz/rock sound of the band Chicago
So, his immersion in virtuoso guitarists
Like Larry Carlton of the Crusaders made sense.

When my brother caught wind of a Crusaders concert
At the Cellar Door in D.C.,
He grabbed me and a mutual friend of ours,
And the three of us trekked to D.C. to see the band.

The Cellar Door in Georgetown was a premier club;
Small and intimate; every seat had a clear view of the stage
Which meant you could see what your heroes were playing.

It was a great show, the band was great, and Carlton was superb.
My brother and I would go back to the Cellar Door
To see Rickie Lee Jones a few years before the club closed.

He and I eventually circled back to the rock we adored.
Fusion was just a phase for me but a powerful one
That kept me happily sidetracked for several years.

With My Tail Between My Legs

The year was 1976. I was nineteen years old.
I found a fourth-floor walkup on 3400 St. Paul Street,
In a quaint old building on the east side of Johns Hopkins University.

My new digs had two rooms and a bathroom.
The main room had a small kitchenette with a stove, fridge, and sink,
And in the other, a bedroom with a small closet.
The windows in both rooms opened out to St. Paul Street.

One of the most liberating aspects of my newfound freedom
Was inviting my girlfriend over to frolic without curtains or rules,
Walk around naked, and leave my paraphernalia out in the open.

She was a dark-haired beauty, an earthy *splendida,* who came
To comfort me on my first night of willing captivity,
And make sure everything was put in its proper place.

She and I traversed across the infinite expanse of a California King;
A bed I inherited from my grandfather's furniture purge.
We smoked hash, drank, laughed, and carried on
In a manner not unlike the Hebrews when they fled Egypt.

My exodus also included my own set of idols:
Books, albums, my prized stereo,
Some assorted clothes, and the minimum required
To keep my skinny, 6-foot, 160-pound frame watered and fed.

When I found myself alone and left to my own devices,
I would take in foreign films at the Playhouse on 25th Street
Then walk back to my apartment lost in thought.

Larry Levy

But paradise only lasted three months
As all the money I had saved was quickly spent.
So, as punishment I returned home with my tail between my legs.

Record and Tape Collector

The first place I bought long playing records
Was at Hecht Company in the Reisterstown Road Plaza.
The record department was street level
On the bottom floor of the store.

They used an A-F pricing method that became more expensive
As you made your way further into the alphabet.
The selection usually revolved around currently released LP's
Although they did carry full libraries of more well-known bands.

I bought many albums there as a youngster
Including one of my all-time favorites,
"Let it Bleed" by The Rolling Stones.

When For the Record opened midway between Hecht's and Stewart's,
I bought my first two classical LP's there:
"The Complete Piano Preludes" by Sergei Rachmaninoff
And Bach's "Brandenburg Concertos."

In 1976, when I moved into my first apartment on St. Paul Street,
One of my favorite things to do was walk down to Cold Spring Lane
And visit my favorite record store, Record and Tape Collector.

They had a fantastic collection of reasonably priced records.
I always found what I was looking for in all genres of music
And unlike Hecht's, they played great music while you shopped.

Across the street from the recessed Record and Tape building
Was Soundscape, an up-scale stereo store with all the latest gear.
Now I had two places to spend the bread I didn't have.

Larry Levy

When I moved back to Chokeberry Road after my money ran out,
I would drive up to Record and Tape Collector
If I heard an album I had to have.

I began to migrate to Record and Tape Trader
When they opened a store in Pikesville next to Gordon's Crabs.
The Towson store became the biggest and best of them all.

And even when competitors like Chick's Legendary, Music Machine,
Andie Music, and the Record Theater opened their doors for business,
I always bought most of my records at Record and Tape Collector.

The 45

The 45-record loomed large in my musical history.
Strangely, it began by discarding them with a kid who lived
Across the street from me in Tamarac court.

The woods behind his house were good for all kinds of boy things:
Catching salamanders and crayfish, shooting BB guns,
Letting off bombs, and throwing 45's.

He was one year older than me and went to a different school.
Since he had an older brother and sister,
He was able to get his hands on tons of 45's, ripe for the chucking.

The records came undressed with no jackets
And the needle having left a scar;
Making them the perfect candidates to dispose of improperly.
We pitched them one-by-one from the side, with a flick of the wrist.

After the first day of taking fun to new heights,
I recruited my younger brother to take part in the action.
He and I watched 7" disks climb to the heavens
Then tumble and fall like Top 40 fame.

The trees that shaded my neighbor's house
And divided his yard from Pikesville Senior High
Became a graveyard for rock 'n roll.

II.

When my mom needed to go out to Westview Mall on Route 40
My brother and I were quick to ask if we could go
Because there was a store called Music House that sold only 45's.

The large store was rectangularly shaped, open in the middle,
With floor to ceiling record bins on both walls.
They had every 45, new and old, even obscure artists and bands.

My brother and I were in musical heaven.
When my mom returned from shopping,
She had to drag us out of the store
After paying the bill for what was our first, but not last, vice.

I learned the various labels representing my favorite bands.
The Beatles had the Capitol red and orange label,
The Stones, London blue and white.
Many artists were on the red Columbia label,
While Creedence Clearwater Revival
Donned the distinctive green and orange Fantasy label.

III.

In my younger days, Drug Fair in the Greenspring Shopping Center
Had a luncheonette which was the go-to spot for French fries
After a fun Saturday of roller skating at Wellwood Elementary.
It was also a repository of paper clips and rubber bands
For all the battles my mates and I had behind the bowling alley.

They also sold 45's on the right-hand side as you entered the store.
For sixty-nine cents I was able to cure my 'Pop Fever'
Within walking distance from Chokeberry Road.

There was also a cute girl with wild black hair who worked there
And lived across the street on Smith Avenue.
For some reason our paths never crossed all through senior high.

We talked about school, music, and whether she got a discount.
I was glad to finally meet her and dismayed that it took so long.
I left the store relieved that all was still well in Wellwood.

IV.

But 1974 saw the peak of popularity for the 45.
It was all downhill for the quick-spinning single after that.
No exclusive 45-record store or pretty girl from Drug Fair
Could save the 7" disc.

The LP was already dominant but now the cassette came into vogue.
Home recordings and bootlegs became very popular.
The Sony Walkman added mobility and in-dash cassette players
Became standard in every car rolling off the assembly line.

Then a new disc rolled into town: the CD.
Brimming with a shiny surface, promises of higher fidelity,
And a century-long lifespan,
The compact disc now replaced analog with digital.

When I moved into my first apartment,
My 45-collection sadly did not accompany me.

But there will always be a soft spot in my heart
For the two-song record with the groove worn popular track
And the hidden gem on the flip side.

Larry Levy

The Tape Wars

In the world of tape, the reel-to-reel machine was king.
After all, the Beatles' "Sgt. Peppers" was recorded on one –
(Actually two 4-track machines) --
And it doesn't get much better than that!

The cassette was a miniaturized version of the reel to reel
And offered convenience in a compact form.
Machines recorded and played back at 1 7/8 I.P.S. (inch-per-second),
And suffered in quality compared to their bigger brother.

Then there was the 8-track that offered the additional convenience
Of not having to flip the tape over to listen or record tracks.
But the quality was inferior to the cassette.

My grandfather knew, my brother knew, and I knew:
The cassette was where it was at!

In fact, everyone I was friends with had cassettes –
In their homes and later in their cars.
I never knew anyone that had an 8-track machine
Until I left the ghetto of Wellwood.

In my early years, I would walk around the neighborhood
And travel to Wildwood with my prized Norelco 150 cassette player.
It was one of the joys of my young life.

Then I graduated to a Panasonic cassette player
That had AM/FM and could record internally from the radio.
This was a profound technological advancement.

My brother and I would call WCAO on Park Heights Avenue
And ask Johnny Dark to play the long version of the Doors'
"Light My Fire" so we could record it on the Panasonic.

Still Well In Wellwood

As things advanced and home audio subdivided into
An AM/FM receiver, turntable, and speakers,
The advent of the separate cassette recorder became a necessity.

Once cars came into the picture, a cassette player in the glove box
And speakers under the rear window became the logical next step.
I would record tapes at home from the radio, LP records, and 45's,
And then play them in my car as I was rockin' down the road.

Then came the portability of the Sony Walkman –
A cassette player you could take anywhere –
Including the most coveted places of all, pool-side and the beach.

The quality of cassette tapes improved dramatically
With the advent of metal and CR02, (chromium dioxide tape).
One more dagger in the heart of the 8-track.

The 8-track hung out for a while and won a few battles
Particularly in cars in the mid 70's.
But the cassette won the war.

Larry Levy

The House Painter

Our home on Chokeberry was bought in 1958.
It was a red-brick split-level with wood shingles on both sides
And across the back of the house.

After eighteen years the shingles were in bad need of painting.
My dad figured I could use the money
And offered me 250 bucks to paint the entire house.

He would buy the paint and all the supplies
As well as procure a ladder that extended up to the roof.
I was the labor.

I began on the kitchen side where I didn't need a ladder
And finished half of one side on the first day.
I was already counting the money and what I would buy with it.

When I came back the next morning to check on my work,
And show my dad how good a job I'd done,
The side of the house looked as though I had used invisible paint.

The shingles were so dried out they literally ate up everything,
And from my father's perspective not dissimilar
To what my brother, sister, and I did to his food supply.
All the work I had done the day before was for naught.

My dad said I would need to do two or three coats,
To account for the aging process that took place over the years
Even though that part of the deal was never discussed.

I was turned off to the job right away and never would have agreed
If I knew I had to paint the house three times.
So, I asked a friend of mine who lived on Chippewa Drive for help.
We would split the $250 and finish the job in a couple of days.

Still Well In Wellwood

He accepted my offer and came ready to work the next day.
When my father caught wind of the deal
He went mental and dug deep into his bag of cliches.

"If you spent more time just doing a job
Instead of trying to think how to get out it,
You'd be much better off."

My friend was summarily dismissed with my apologies.
He didn't understand what the big deal was, and neither did I.
But my dad was the one holding the cards so I had no choice.

After my friend went home and the barbs thrown at me ceased,
We came to a revised agreement.
I would paint the entire house one time for $125;
And he would do the second coat and a third if needed.

I finished painting the house in one week
Without any mess or accidents.
He gave me the $125 in cash as promised.

But unfortunately, he spent most of the summer painting the house.
I felt sorry for him so I refrained from revealing
That I spent the money on records, pot, and then wasted the rest.

Larry Levy

Frustration 101

There were two reasons I enrolled at Loyola College:
They had a Russian language program
And the building where English classes were taught
Looked like something out of Medieval England.

I signed up for Introduction to Russian, Poly Sci,
And decided to take a class in Shakespeare
Along with Victorian and Edwardian poetry.

During winter break I got a-wild hair for accounting
Wherein my father broke into a Cossack dance;
A nice gesture considering my interest in Russian culture.

But I was bored to tears with debits and credits
So, I dropped the class after a few weeks.

My father stood up from his Gopak 'squat dance' and bellowed:
"What the hell are you going to do with your life?"

I responded by going back to my old ways,
And immediately signed up for a studio art class
Where nude models gave me hope and inspiration.

And just as drawing them was a poor substitute
For the desire they engendered,
Another year of college brought me no closer
To being able to solve another of life's riddles:
How to make a living doing something you love.

Studio Art

In the 5th grade, I befriended a guy who lived
In the Pickwick apartments on Sanzo Road.
He was somewhat shy and reserved
And an excellent artist by the age of eleven.

I remember being impressed with his drawings
And how quickly he could render a figure or landscape.
While I was busy throwing baseballs at people, he was drawing them.

I had "ants-in-my-pants" as my dad used to say,
So, sports and fast-moving activities was where it was at for me.
My friend and I went our separate ways but his influence remained.

In senior year at Pikesville, I signed up for an art class,
And made a clay figurine of a nude woman with long hair.
From a seated position I bent her torso forward and covered her face
As her arms wrapped around the tops of her knees.

When I rolled the clay between my fingers, I experienced her sadness.
As she began to take shape and come to life in my hands,
I felt myself becoming emotionally connected to something I created.

After my woman was completed, I turned a piece of walnut
On a lathe in woodshop so she could sit in comfort.
When I moved from apartment to apartment, she came with me;
Her home on top of my dresser.

In the spring of 1977, I took a studio art class at Loyola College,
That once again tickled my imagination
In a way that strict academics could never elicit.

I learned how to draw from live models,
Which meant capturing the essence of the form quickly

Larry Levy

And not getting bogged down in detail.
I fought against what I thought was an on-the-spot performance
And did poorly with this aspect of drawing.

When our instructor gave us home assignments,
And used the words "spontaneous" and "immediate"
I ignored her suggestions and drew from photographs instead.

First came pencil copies of a Degas nude
Followed by the face and torso of a young woman.
My last composition was a pen and ink of St. Basil's Cathedral.

My teacher liked my work
But as it was obvious that I worked from photographs,
She dropped me to a "B" for ignoring the purpose of the assignment.

She was a great instructor and I didn't care about the grade.
What mattered to me was that fine art found a place
In the turnstile of self-expression that was my life at the time.

I also learned there was a certain peace in drawing;
In the process of the work itself
And the aftereffects from long and contemplative visual study.

And though I was still unable to replicate
What my friend in the 5th grade understood at age eleven,
I discovered my own kind of freedom.

The Cost of Freedom

The other tail I brought home along with me,
After my first taste of independence failed,
Belonged to Connie, a beautiful Afghan hound
I acquired during my first month on St. Paul Street.

Connie and I were put on double probation.
She had two strikes against her: she was female and a purebred.
My father accused her of mental instability
And blamed the browning of his prized front yard grass on her
Because "everyone knows female urine is caustic."

When his favorite son, Rocky II,
A high-strung mix of unknown breeds with an eagerness to bite,
Began chomping down on everything that moved,
Connie was accused of elitism and female trickery.

I had even more strikes against me.
My first misdemeanor was the console piano I brought home
And placed right smack dab in the living room
Where my dad's Motorola blasted out the hits from 1950.

I pounded the keys for hours on end
Causing my father even more aggravation.
Then came his constant refrain of, *"pianissimo, pianissimo!"*
That was an imminent threat to my 'forte per usual.'

I was serious about school which he endorsed
But from his perspective, I took all the wrong courses:
English, Philosophy, and Music.

I worked six days a week part time
But my socialist leanings made me a radical in his eyes
And kept my status as a vagabond intact.

Larry Levy

I came in late at night and slept well into the morning.
When he went to work to scratch out a living
I was getting high with the maid
Which meant neither she nor I did anything productive.

"You think you can do whatever you want
Whenever you want to do it!"
The thesis of the book, my dad, and many other fathers
Had always wanted to write but never had the time
Because they were too busy enforcing the rules.

After ninety days of autonomy
I found it difficult to return to the military operation at home.
But it was his house.
He was right, I was right, and we were both wrong.

I learned that freedom wasn't free, but man, it sure was freeing.

First Beer

In the front seats of my guitar player friend's white Opel wagon,
The two of us sat and listened to music, came up with material,
And talked about girls, bands, cars, and things that went fast.

But in music as in life one must be open to new friends.
And the new friend that found its way into our repertoire was beer.
At nineteen, I was a little late to the game but a quick learner.

My alcohol virginity was lost on a hot summer night in 1976
When we pulled onto a side street from Milford Mill Road,
Parked between two vacant cars, and began indulging.

My first beer of all things, was a heavy Heineken dark.
I remember how 'bready' it tasted, how filling it was,
And how different the buzz felt from pot.

We sat there for a few hours, drinking, laughing,
And listening to cassettes of our band rehearsals
To see what songs worked and which ones needed to be replaced.

After we each had three beers, we were feeling hungry
And the Burger King on Reisterstown Road across from the Plaza
Was calling our name.

No sooner did we park the car
Then I opened the door and puked in the parking lot.
Fifteen minutes later, my friend and I
Went inside and ordered a couple of whoppers.

Most people associate their first 'anything' with a positive memory.
And even though Heineken lager is still my favorite of all time,
I gave up the dark side of things, with beer anyway.

Larry Levy

The White Bird

The next car I bought for myself after parting with the MG *Midget*
Also came via the classified section of *The Baltimore Sun.*
The seller lived off Falls Road in Hampden.

For $1300 I picked up a 1968 Pontiac *Firebird* convertible.
Though white was not my color of choice,
The black 'rag top' provided a nice contrast
To the sexy shape of the chassis.

My MG, though fun to drive, had a low-powered 4-cylinder engine
While the 8-cylinder *Firebird* packed 350 horsepower.
It had impressive pickup and was smooth as silk on the highway.

But for me it was all about the appearance, the lines.
The *Firebird* was so good looking with the top down
I found more enjoyment staring at it than driving it.

Every Saturday night my father would ask me for the keys to the car.
He was out in the dating world after he and my mom split up
And his green 4-door Dodge *Dart* wasn't cutting it with the ladies.

He and I developed a tacit agreement about the car:
"If you borrow the 'Bird' for your galivanting pleasure,
I'm having friends over to jam in the basement."
I left out the part about smoking pot and girls spending the night.

The Pontiac was a good mate for about a year.
There were two flaws about the *Firebird* that were a bummer:
The power steering made for terrible handling
And the car would 'bottom out' riding over the smallest of bumps.
Plus, the rear wheel wells were rusting out and expensive to replace.
I sold the car for $1200 so, I basically broke even.

Unusual Cargo

I had been delivering newspapers by car for quite some time,
Needed the income to fund my various vices,
And was thrilled not having a boss look over my shoulder.

But "everything in life is compromise" as my dad would say.
If I wanted to be an 'independent contractor' and use my own car,
Then maintenance was a reality I had to accept.

When the very newspaper that I had been delivering
Made its way to my front door on Chokeberry Road,
Along with the invaluable classified section.,
I thought I had struck gold.

At the end of the "Help Wanted" section in the morning *'Sun'*
Was the answer to my newfound conundrum:
"Driver Wanted: Good Pay, Flexible Hours,
Car Provided, Apply Within."

I got up from the kitchen table and gave the white rotary phone a spin.
The job was on Liberty Road in Randallstown
And if I could be there by 10am, the job was mine.

"And on the first day, God said, "Let there be light!"

And on the first day my new boss said:
"Okay, today I want you to drive the rabbi around
And go wherever he wants to go.
He is here from Israel and is collecting for his synagogue back home.
And while you're driving, take this tape, you might learn something."

I took my place in his block-long, brown, station wagon.
I looked at my Hassidic passenger with the black hat, full beard,

Larry Levy

Spiral notebook with all the places he and I were about to go,
And wondered if this ride was going to be a blessing or a curse.

All I could think about was, "if my family, friends,
And anyone I went to school with could see me now,
Would I still be able to get a date on Saturday night?"

I was respectful, spoke when I was spoken to,
And kept my eyes on the road.
The rabbi would call out an address, and I'd turn the wagon
In the direction of his next donor.

When he disappeared into the first building,
I played the tape my boss gave me.
A guy in a deep baritone voice started singing in Hebrew
Which is when I popped in my Black Sabbath tape,
Masters of Reality just for perspective.

After the rabbi made a few stops,
I was ready for lunch and asked if I could stop and get something.
"We only have a few more place to go.
You can hold out!" he said authoritatively.
So, a trip to Burger Chef was not to be.

To make amends for my departure from the rigors of the faith
I offered as sacrifice my orthodox grandmother
For my sin of non-kosher temptations.
Our last stop was her apartment.

When I opened the outside door to her building
My diminutive, 4'10", 90 lb. grandmother
Was coming up the basement steps carrying her laundry.

She looked up and saw her eldest grandson with a rabbi.
The sunlight was coming through the glass of the front door
Much the same as when Moses saw God.

Still Well In Wellwood

I swallowed hard when I heard angelic singing
But returned to normal functioning when it turned out to be
A Streisand record coming from a neighbor's open window.

My grandmother excitedly opened her apartment door, let us both in,
And wrote out a check for seventy-five dollars.
Then she hugged and kissed me and for some odd reason
Began dancing like 'Granny' from *The Beverly Hillbillies*.

And just as I was heading back to the place where it all began,
I saw my brother in his light blue Dodge *Dart*
Passing me on the other side of Smith Avenue.

He didn't recognize me because my friend with the black hat
Was not something he associated with his freaky brother.
Later that evening, I recanted the story to both he and my dad
To a chorus of laughter, barbs, and biblical interpretations.

I guess in the scheme of things I was lucky.
I didn't have to provide 'muscle' in case the rabbi had to run for it.
After all, he was collecting for a good cause,
Not threatening someone that didn't pay their gambling debt.

And on the second day, I quit!

Larry Levy

Salmon Cakes

From her orthopedic shoes to the crown of her saintly head,
My 4'10", 90-lb grandmother was the strongest woman I ever met.
"Her greatest strength was in the kitchen" my father would say.

Every Wednesday night, we would go over to her apartment
For our weekly Kosher meal and to spend some time with her.
She lived alone and our visit was the highlight of her week.

I was not a fan of her cooking although I loved her baking;
Mostly sweets like chocolate cookies and breakfast buns.
Some of her dinner meals wreaked havoc on my gut.

But out of fairness, it was difficult to be a good Kosher cook
Particularly when my brother, sister, and I
Favored Burger Chef and Gordon's Crabs.

As a kid I was mostly pliable and cooperative.
I listened to her stories about the different places she used to live
And how good of a boy my father was growing up;
That was until his records of conduct at school were uncovered.

When I'd spend the night, she'd give me coffee milk
From the same cup my father used to drink out of as a kid:
The sugar stirred with a silver spoon made in Russia from 1880.

I loved breakfast because I was so hungry
After not eating for nearly twelve hours
And because there was less 'kosher-ness' to the meal.

She made my favorite, fried matzoh,
Topped with a shovel full of cinnamon and sugar.

Then when I went home a few hours later,
Having eaten the equivalent of four sheets of cardboard,
I couldn't go to the bathroom for a week.

My mother had to intervene and put the kibosh on the consumption
Of all products containing unleavened bread
Despite thousands of years of historical precedence.

As I grew more rebellious and pickier in general,
I tried more progressive ways of eating – enter vegetarianism.

But cooler heads prevailed and we came up with a compromise.
I promised to be a little more open to a varied diet
If she would lay off the rendered chicken fat known as s*chmaltz*–
The supposed flavorful ingredient even the chicken didn't want.

I began eating my dad's favorite, veal pocket,
Which quite frankly tasted like any other pocket you might consume–
Levi's, Wrangler, Eddie Bauer.
I picked around the strange consistency of meat
And whenever in doubt, used tons of ketchup.

One week after that *delicious* meal
My grandmother gave me bag full of goodies –
Chocolate cookies made by hand that I adored.
I came home and put them on the counter for future eating.

My grandmother phoned every day when I was at work
And left messages to please call her back.
There was something of the utmost importance she had to tell me.

Finally, my father left a message with me,
In a voice like God almighty,
"Call your grandmother!"
I made the call during work when the entire office went to lunch.

Larry Levy

The conversation went like this:

"Why haven't you called me, I was worried sick?"

"I'm sorry Gram, I was tied up this week – what's going on?"

"I have to apologize."

"For what?"

"Listen, you know that bag I gave you last week?"

"Yes"

"And I said it was your favorite chocolate cookies."

"Yes. yes"

"Well, it wasn't, they were salmon cakes. I'm so sorry."

"It's okay – no big deal."

Then came the lightning bolt of guilt.

"Can you ever forgive me?"

"Yes, of course. Listen, I gotta run, I'm at work – I'll see you on Wednesday night."

"Okay. I'll give you your cookies then. Make sure you don't forget to come."

I called my father and he laughed himself silly.
When I got home, I immediately threw out the bag on the counter.

Still Well In Wellwood

Fortunately, in Jewish law (somewhere in fine print),
It is strictly forbidden to have hostage exchange.
I picked up the real cookies on Wednesday
And no one was the wiser.

Larry Levy

From a Trip to a Fall

During senior year of high school
My bandmates and I from Sweet Cider
Went to the Randallstown movie theatre on Liberty Road
For a special triple-feature performance of The Beatles.

On tap were *Help*, *Yellow Submarine*, and *Let it Be*.
Help was all fun and games and good old rock 'n roll;
Yellow Submarine was a psychedelic masterpiece,
And *Let it Be* featured the famous NYC rooftop performance.

At the stroke of midnight, a wild mix of aficionados and heads
Sat mesmerized in front of the big screen
As floor-to-ceiling quad speakers
Introduced us to a new way of listening to music.

At 5am, after the movies let out,
Scores of wide-eyed psychedelic induced teenagers were let loose
In the Liberty Plaza parking lot to replay the experience just realized.
My friends and I laughed and carried on and walked around the mall.

On the other side of the street, across from the theater,
The words Randallstown Music caught my eye;
A music store I never knew existed.
The seed was planted on that highly-charged pre-dawn Sunday Morn.

Two years later when I was in the market for a piano,
I went back to Randallstown Music in Liberty Plaza.
The fond memory of seeing the Beatles
From behind rose-colored glasses led me to their doorstep.

After checking out quite a few catalogs,
I special ordered a new console piano.

Still Well In Wellwood

I had the piano delivered to 3400 St. Paul Street
Where it sat in the main room of my efficiency apartment.
I played every day until my bank account was depleted.

When I moved back home to Chokeberry Road,
 I set the piano up in the living room and continued with my passion
Until it was time for the piano to be tuned.

When the piano tuner came to my house,
He informed me that the sound board was defective
And had to be replaced before it could be properly tuned.

The owner of Randallstown Music did the right thing.
He arranged to pick up the piano and off to the factory it went.
Six months later she returned good as new
But in her absence, I had gone back to my first love, drums.

Rock 'n roll, always ready to dig her claws into me,
Called me back to the basement with brother and company
To get down to the business of forming a band.

The date was July 7th, 1977 or numerically, 7/7/77,
A date that for me would live in musical instrument infamy.
 I went back to Randallstown Music for more punishment.

I was lured into a buying a set of used drums,
In the beautiful and less often seen sky blue pearl finish.
I immediately drove them to their new home on Chokeberry Road.

About a month later, during band practice,
I leaned onto the floor tom, elbow to drum head,
And within a few seconds the drum collapsed as I fell forward.

Larry Levy

When I got up to survey the damage
I noticed that beneath the speckled gray paint on the interior shell
Was a drum completely constructed with particle board.

This of course meant the entire drum set
Was made from the same flimsy material.
The floor tom was destroyed and the drums as a set were worthless.
I sold off the remainder of the set piece by piece to recoup my loss.

I realized it was not the owner of the music store who was at fault.
Nor was it just coincidence or bad luck.
It was clearly the demise of American products and workmanship.
I wasn't fully aware then but 'the fall' had already begun.

A New Sound

In the Spring of 10th grade, I was well-versed
In the music of the Beatles, Rolling Stones, and most Brit bands.
I was also an avid follower of the west coast psychedelic scene.

But my entire musical vocabulary was about to be expanded
By a guy who lived down the street on Chokeberry
Directly across from my gal pal's rancher.

His father was a dentist who in the 5th grade
Came to Wellwood Elementary to teach us about oral hygiene,
And espouse the virtues of chewing Dentyne gum after every meal.
He was a hit with the ADD and oral fixation crowd.

His son and I were friends from the early days at Wellwood.
We met up a few times to smoke cigs at a giant rock
That separated the woods from the baseball field at Pikesville Sr.

But on a beautiful spring day in 1972
He invited me over his house and into his bedroom
To hear the Allman Brother's double LP, *Live at Fillmore East*.
We listened to all four sides as he played the role of D.J.,
And blew my mind with the expansive Atlanta based sound.

The record completely changed my way of thinking
And marked a turning point in my understanding
Of what music could be.

It was around this time I started playing drums.
Of course, the Allman Brothers were technically beyond my grasp,
But in time, I knew my hands and feet would catch up.

Over the next year or two, my speed and reaction time improved
As I learned how to improvise on rapidly changing musical themes.

Larry Levy

The parties and jam sessions that became more frequent
Now featured Allman Brother's songs like "Statesboro Blues"
"Stormy Monday" and "In Memory of Elizabeth Reed."

I would go to Allman Brother's concerts whenever the chance arose
And seeing them live 'in-the-round' at Painter's Mill
Was one of the highlights of my musical life.
They were fantastic even without the great Duane Allman.

My love affair with the band began
On that fateful day in my friend's bedroom,
Never to be forgotten and always appreciated.

The Band Without a Name

A guitar player friend of mine
Kept my feet firmly planted
In the muck and mire of rock 'n roll.

He lived the lifestyle; ate terrible food from 7-11,
Drank and smoked and stayed up all hours of the night.
But he was also an excellent player
And 100% committed to his instrument and performance.

He'd hear about a party, somewhere, anywhere,
Bribe me with weed and the promise of chicks,
If I would pack up my Ludwig's and join him.

Our playing was spontaneous.
Without any idea of where the music would go
We would improvise around a basic theme and then take solos.

The hangers on dug it, were as stoned as we were,
And thrilled that live musicians were playing
In their living room or backyard.

We eventually started a band
And practiced at the singer's house in Belair
Over the Maryland state line in Pennsylvania.

We worked out some complicated songs;
"She's a Dancer" by Crack the Sky,
And "The Ocean" by Led Zeppelin.

But the band with no name ended as quick as it began.

Larry Levy

The Parties, Five

There were five major parties
That helped shape my Wellwood years.

I.

The first was back in grade school.
A fun and funny girl who lived on Copperfield Road
Organized a dance party for about twenty kids.

She had all the essentials: a basement, no parental supervision,
And most of the current 45's heard on AM radio.
She played hostess, DJ, and understated matchmaker.

"These Eyes" by The Guess Who was the selection
That prompted me to ask this girl to slow dance.
She was as pretty, as she was nice, and a pleasure to hold.

The pitter-patter that moved from her heart to mine,
And the new, unexplained flush I felt all over,
Kept me rooted in the mystery.

I had never thought about her in a 'steady' sort of way
Nor did I really take notice of her in school.
But the song combined with all that touching and closeness
Made me start to see this whole girl thing in a different light.

II.

A new girl late on the scene in the Wellwood years
Lived on Old Court Road, a few houses from Stevenson Road.
She had a rancher with a built-in pool in her backyard.

I'm not sure how she chose the kids that would attend
But boy was I grateful that I was included.

She and I got along swimmingly as it were,
And along with another newbie from Fort Garrison Elementary,
The two were the new cool girls at Wellwood.

There was an even mix of boys and girls
Splashing around and going down the sliding board
Which for me was novel because at my grandfather's pool
Sliding boards were considered too dangerous.

But any great party even as a kid needed a certain amount of danger.
The result: more girls being asked to go steady.
When you put boys and girls together in and around a pool
Something magical happens.

III.

The next cool shindig also took place around a pool.
This time it was in junior high midway
Between all the Bar and Bat Mitzvah dances.

The hostess and I went to first grade together at Beth Tfiloh.
When she reemerged from Ft. Garrison in seventh grade,
She immediately became the 'it' girl at Pikeville Jr.

She was very good looking and had a way about her
That drew people into her orbit.
All the boys loved her.

She lived on the corner of Keyser and Stevenson Road
In a beautiful house with giant bay windows
That sat elevated and recessed from the street.

Larry Levy

In the backyard was an in-ground swimming pool.
The boys went in first, usually by way of cannonballs or goofy dives,
And girls screamed when they were thrown in completely dressed.

When the hostess decided it was time to do something else,
She put on records and everyone went inside to dance.
Most of us were still dripping wet from the pool.

There was something remarkably different and appealing
About seventh grade girls in bikinis who were just beginning
To assert the power of their attractiveness.
Learning was never so much fun.

IV.

The next party took place years later in high school.
A friend of mine called a spontaneous gathering
In his home one hot summer night in the summer of 1972.

In order to pull something off that quick you need two things:
A lot of friends and a push button phone to get the word out fast.
He had both.

We had hung out a few times he and I,
And were just beginning to become friends.
I assumed it was why I was invited.

He lived in Indian Village, walking distance from Chokeberry
Which meant I didn't need a ride in case things got out of hand.
His parents were away so we had the place to ourselves.

There were about a dozen of us hanging out in his basement;
A wild bunch of guys competing for crazy
Until the wee hours of the morning.

The next day we got up, moaned, and went our separate ways.
No one talked about the party much
Because no one remembered much of what went on.
The sign of a good party.

V.

But it was the party a few years after high school had ended
That a quiet and diminutive figure,
Organized well in advance to ring in the new year.

He lived on Carla Road, a mere stone's throw from Pikesville Sr.
And asked our band of misfits to play in his basement.
No sooner had we worked our way through a few numbers,
Then the volume of people began to swell throughout the house.

The place was packed!

There were friends there I hadn't seen for years including the host;
Those home on break from college
And all the Wellwood-hangers-on like me that stayed behind.

We played from early evening until well into the middle of the night.
When the sun came up on a brand, new year
There were bodies in various stages of sleep
Strewn from basement to top floor and everywhere in between.

A group of us walked out of the house
Shook hands and thanked the host who we all said had,
"Thrown the greatest party of all time."

My friend from Chokeberry and leader of the neighborhood
Waved goodbye and climbed into his brown Plymouth *Duster*.
I never saw him again.

Larry Levy

A Fair Weathered Friend

One day, on a beautiful sunny May afternoon,
I was driving alone in my 1968 Dodge *Coronet*,
Minding my own business without a care in the world.
In fact, I was whistling.

I had just made a left-hand turn from Belair Road onto Joppa Road
When off to my left was the most gorgeous car I had ever seen
Parked in front of a small dealership sitting parallel to the street.

I pulled into the lot and beelined right up to the car.
Within ten seconds a salesman came over to greet me
With his fishing rod and bait prepared to reel me in.

First, he gave me the facts and figures:
"What we have here is a white 1970, Dodge *Challenger* coupe
With custom painted black lines, stock wheels, and whitewall tires.
She's got a 340, 8 cylinder, 4-bbl carburetor under the hood.
Inside, black bucket seats and a console with a 3-spd automatic."

Then came the scratch and tickle, the offer that never fails:
"So, would you like to take her for a spin?"
"Sure" I said, and soon we were cruising down
The backroads on our way to heaven.

The car drove like a dream and handled better than my '68 *Firebird*.
The black interior was in perfect shape
And the seats cuddled me like a newborn babe.

He asked me, "So, are you into fast cars" to which I replied,
"No, I'm into beautiful cars and this is one beautiful car, man!"

The *Challenger*, minus the black stripes, was the exact same car
Featured in the 1971 movie, "Vanishing Point".

The salesman was a nice guy, spoke my lingo: rock 'n roll, girls, cars,
And knocked the price down to $2200 without my asking.
I signed the contract and drove off into the sunset.
I came back the next day to retrieve my beater *Coronet*.

It was a great summer with my new wheels.
I drove my favorite roads in Northern Baltimore County
Hitting all the parallel avenues that took me deep into the country:
Greenspring Avenue, Park Heights Avenue, and Falls Road.

On my way back, I turned from Falls Road onto Hillside;
The same road I took nearly every day during high school.
Still there on three successive telephone poles
Were the simple but profound words left by the spray-paint prophet:
"Sex, Drugs, Rock 'n Roll."

Hillside was for most the gateway drug to parties at 'The Meadow.'
For others, it was a shortcut to various destinations.
But for me it was where the sun broke through the trees in fragments
And tripped-out my eyes and imagination with glissandos of light.

When winter came my trouble with the muscle car began.
The engine would not turn over even on days with relatively no wind.
My mechanic spoke of the woes of 4-bbl carburetors
And no matter what I tried the damn car wouldn't start.

I sold the *Challenger* for $1700
To an excited 17-year-old a few days before Christmas.
As I watched the car disappear into the falling snow,
I learned my lesson about fair weathered friends.

Larry Levy

My Inspiration

If rock 'n roll was the greatest thing ever invented
Then most certainly playing drums was a strong second,
Followed by the need to make noise with others
Therefore, completing the circle of what rock 'n roll was all about.

Although my father's perpetual cry of, "why here, why always here?"
Convinced him there was evidently no God,
In truth, my musician friends and I did play elsewhere.

If he only knew some of the places we played,
And what we did as preparation before we played,
He would have had even less hair on his tortured scalp.

The best gig we procured was a Bar Mitzvah party
At the Holiday Inn on Reisterstown Road and the beltway.
It was close to home; we were paid, fed, and 'watered'
Even though we had to repeat songs to get through the evening.

The hours of practicing in my father's basement paid off.
We sounded good and received many compliments.
Best of all, there was no one there to tell us to "Turn it Down!"

My brother did a great job leading the band on guitar and vocals.
My friend from Waco Court was already an accomplished player
As was the saxophone player who lived up the street
And the bass player who came all the way from Marriottsville.

I remember looking out into the crowd during a Stones' song
And noticed a young boy of thirteen watching my every move.
Even when I'd look away and then back, his eyes were on me.

Still Well In Wellwood

I flashed back to a friend's Bar Mitzvah party I attended as a lad
At the Woodholme Country Club off Reisterstown Road
Where he and I used to play tennis and eat like kings.

On the night of his Bar Mitzvah party
I also watched the drummer the entire night.
It was 1969 and the band was The Continental Rockers.

I stood in the shadows and preferred watching the band
Even though there was plenty of opportunity to dance with girls.
The drummer was fantastic and left a lasting impression.

I was hoping the kid watching me had the same experience
And that if I in some way could make a difference in his life
The gig would all be worth it.

Years later, that boy became my inspiration for teaching drums.

One Way, San Diego

In February of 1978, I decided it was time
To move away and start over.

A friend of mine from Pikesville
Was going to San Diego State University
And La Jolla seemed like an attractive option.

I filled one small suitcase with clothes, some cash,
And as a gift, a single-barrel carburetor
For my friend's slant-6 Dodge *Dart*.

I purchased a one-way ticket,
Sold off my prized stereo equipment
To my baseball buddy who lived in Chokeberry Court,
And boarded an airplane for the first time.

My friend picked me up at the airport
And drove us back to his apartment
Where the living room floor now became my bed.

For breakfast we went to The Big Kitchen on Grape Street,
Where Whoopi Goldberg worked when she was first starting out.
A fab hang with great food.

The San Diego Zoo was great fun and an adventure.
Despite the incredible amount of walking,
To see animals in their natural habitat was well worth the effort.

We went to Black's Beach, a clothes optional beach in La Jolla,
An eye-opening experience to say the least.
Then it was off to dinner at The Marine Room where waves crashed
Against the glass windows of the restaurant.

Still Well In Wellwood

We drove east out to Juliet, walked around the quaint town,
And took pictures of the beautiful landscape.

Another day we went down to Tijuana,
Went shopping where everything was ridiculously cheap,
And had tacos from a street vendor -- the best I ever had!

One day I went with him to school and while he was in class
I sat in the library and wrote his English paper
To show my appreciation for being a great host and putting me up.

The thought of transferring to SDSU was appealing
But I knew there was no way my dad would spring for the tuition
Or support me in such an adventure.

So, I wrote every day while my friend was in class,
Trying to journal my way through
All the problems I left behind in Baltimore.

After two weeks of intense soul searching
I realized that I didn't need to leave home to begin again.
So, it was back to Wellwood to assert my independence.

Larry Levy

Jeans West

As soon as I returned home from San Diego
I wasted no time in getting a job
And landed one at Jeans West in the Security Square Mall.

I had never worked retail before
But thought selling jeans would be easy
And perhaps a first step into something bigger and better.

My boss was a cool guy that saw in me
Something I never saw in myself
So, his enthusiasm inspired me to work hard.

The job was not without some perks.
Practical girls would flirt for the possibility of a discount,
While the wild ones left their changing room door open.

There was a tall, thin, blond who worked part time
And drove a sexy *MGB* that was so hot
It hurt to look at her.
The girl wasn't bad either.

And while I appreciated these pleasant distractions,
Selling designer jeans and unnecessary accessories
Made me feel completely out of place.
Disco was still in vogue and had no place in my rock 'n roll lifestyle.

One week, the regional manager came into the store every day,
Told us salespeople that our job was to sell, sell, sell,
And follow people around the store until they bought something.

That was all it took for me to realize I was in the wrong profession.
I gave my boss two-week's notice, thanked him for the opportunity,
And left with dignity and my soul intact.

Larry Levy

Milford Mill Swim Club

Milford Mill High was the sister school to Pikesville Senior
And was located on Washington Avenue just off Liberty Road.

I always assumed 'sister school' meant 'the next school over'
Not a reference to an all-girls academy, because if it had,
Me and the boys would have begun
Our intercollegiate studies much earlier.

As it was, I never set foot in Milford Mill High
Except the one time our band, Sweet Cider, played in the gym
On a Saturday night during senior year.

But a few years later after graduation,
I heard about a cool swim club near our sister school
On the other side of Milford Mill at the end of Washington Avenue.

Milford Mill Swim Club, opened in the 50's, and had a rich history.
The quarry was home to a variety of mineral deposits.
I guess scientists who dug archeology had a field day there.

But what scores of teenage kids really dug
Was hearing bands and dancing on *The Buddy Deane Show*
That found its way on TV sets across the country
In the late 50's and early 60's.
Years later, Baltimore directors John Waters and Barry Levenson
Shot scenes for their films, *Cry Baby* and *Liberty Heights* at the club.

When the concrete pond at my grandfather's was no longer a ritual,
I was looking for a new place to swim,
And M.M.S.C. filled the void during the hot summer months.

Still Well In Wellwood

The club was immense and like nothing I had ever seen before.
The main attraction was the giant quarry filled with water
Surrounded by trees and a grass lot that served as a beach.

There was a concession stand for all the insatiable kids,
A picnic area and a change station with bathrooms.
To the left and up a huge hill was an Olympic size pool.

The quarry had a dock with a rope
From which you could propel into the water.
There was also a sectioned off area of lanes for lap swimming
Which is where I spent my time as I was not a 'rope' kind of guy.

Keeping an eye out was the self-appointed guardian of the quarry;
A young guy, in his early twenties, who was there every day
And wore a hat that said, "The Mayor."

He was a nice guy and we became summer friends
But I was glad to be a commoner and just observe his behavior.
I was convinced he took the gig and wore his hat to try and get girls.

I made new friends at the club
Including this beautiful girl from Germany.
She came to M.M.S.C. every day for about two weeks
Before heading back home.
We ended up becoming pen-pals for the next several years.

When I first frequented the club, I went solo.
Then my next-door neighbor joined me which meant getting high
And then driving over to Liberty Road for a stop at Nino Taco
Where Deadheads, hippies, and stoners congregated.

Then I started taking various girlfriends to the club,
Including the girlfriend that became my wife.
She and I stopped going to M.M.S.C. when the concrete pond
At the Hopkins House held more alure.

Larry Levy

3501 Calvert Street

My second way out of Wellwood came to fruition
When I was finally able to afford a place of my own.

I found a great apartment just around the corner
From my first place on St. Paul Street;
A three-floor brick rowhome in Oakenshawe
At 3501 North Calvert Street.

I had the entire third floor to myself:
Two-bedrooms, two-baths, a kitchen, a living area,
And a balcony overlooking a courtyard.

At first, I lived comfortably on my own
But soon realized a roommate
Would cut costs and keep me from moving back home.

I found a Hopkin's medical student who took the second bedroom
And cut my cost down to $200 per month.
I still had an affinity for city life and the Hopkin's University area
Was a desirable place to live.

My father owned Greenway Pharmacy on 34th Street
Right around the corner from my apartment.
During a terrible snowstorm he was forced to spend the night
Because he was unable to drive back to Chokeberry Road.

It was an ironic twist of fate
But I refrained from reading him the riot act
About living under my roof and my rules.

I didn't want to burn any bridges
Just in case I found myself at his doorstep once again.

It's a Maryland Thing

My grandfather loved steamed crabs more than anyone I knew.
He constructed a billiard score-counter to keep track of his intake,
And confided to me that his record was thirty-six large crabs.

He passed down his passion
For the Chesapeake Bay delicacy to his daughter
With strict protocol about what to eat and what to avoid.
My mom passed along his wisdom to my brother, sister, and I.

My father would have nothing to do with the bottom dwellers.
He thought them disgusting and complained about the terrible stench.
So, my mom would only indulge when my dad worked late.

I played pony league baseball at Northwest and Pimlico Jr. High,
And Mr. K's Crab House was the proud sponsor of our team.
So, it was only natural we would get our crustaceans from him.

He was located on Reisterstown Road and Belvedere Ave
On the way to my kosher-keeping grandmother's apartment
From whom the word, 'crab' had to be kept on the down low.

Before we patronized Mr. K's Crab House in the early 70's
We would go to Gordon's on Reisterstown Road in Pikesville.
They had inside dining, and carryout, but we preferred our back porch
Because it was out of sniffing distance from my dad's sensitive nose.

When my mom wanted to treat us kindly and go the distance,
She'd take us to Bo Brooks restaurant on Belair Road.
There we would wait an hour in line to get a table
And eat what were arguably the best steamed crabs in Baltimore.

Larry Levy

In 1978, when I finally decided to get a roommate
To help defray the rent on my apartment,
I chose a Hopkins med student born and raised in Boston.
He only knew from lobsters and had never seen a crab in his life.

One evening when his older brother came to visit him,
The three of us went out to dinner at Bo Brooks.

On the ride over from Calvert Street we smoked a joint
To get primed for some good eats.
They had no idea what to expect.

When we opened the door to the restaurant,
There before our glazed-red eyes
Were dozens of people with mallets hitting these, these, "things."

They stood there motionless laughing at the absurdity of it all.
I must admit, at that moment,
And under those circumstances I agreed with them.

When my novice shell-crackers from the north began eating,
They used their respective mallets with all the grace
Of one of those guys keeping time on a galley ship.

They were not interested in any old school techniques,
Nor could they understand the attraction
Of so much work for so little return.
All I could offer as an explanation was, "It's a Maryland thing."

Still Well In Wellwood

The Civic Center

In my early years, I was friends with a guy who lived on Carla Road
Up the street from the infamous party-thrower.
He was the only person I knew who was into ice hockey.
In fact, he had a wooden air hockey table in his basement.

On two occasions, he and I went to the Civic Center
Across from my favorite novelty store on Baltimore Street,
To watch the Clipper's play.

I was a baseball guy and could not ice skate to save my life.
Wide-eyed and cold, I watched these amazing skaters
Hit this black puck at speeds faster than I could throw.

A few years later, when basketball became more important,
My best friend from Northbrook Road and I went to the Civic Center
And sat courtside to watch the Harlem Globetrotters.

These guys were fabulous athletes, ball handlers, and entertainers.
Plus, they were friendly and interacted with us kids.
Curly Neil was my favorite player because he was fast and funny.
And once my friends learned of my first name,
Curly Neil became my nickname.

In December of 1973, during my junior year at Pikesville,
This pretty girl in the 10th grade who I would see in the hallways,
Asked me if I wanted to go to the Civic Center
To see Emerson, Lake, and Palmer.

Other than the song, "Lucky Man" I didn't care for their music.
But I liked her and hoped the title of the song would do for me
What the lyrics suggested.

Larry Levy

We sat dead center on the floor in the second row.
I put the torn pieces of a paper towel from the bathroom in my ears
Because the band was so unbelievably loud.

And even though I never got lucky in the romantic sense,
We became the best of friends for years.
I leant my ears and heart to her problems with boys, a familiar role,
And she listened to my dreams of becoming
A 19th century Russian artist,
Even though we were living in the 20th century.
I'm not sure who got the shorter end of that stick.

Several years later, after I moved out of Wellwood
And into my new apartment on North Calvert Street,
I returned once again to the Civic Center.

One night, I was sitting ringside at the Pussycat Club
When I saw this girl who reminded me why I was glad to be a guy.
She was someone I could write home about but I lived alone
And was the last person I needed to convince.

I bought her a drink and she immediately began to cry.
I was sure she noticed the giant "S" on my forehead,
But I listened to her stories of heartache and offered my sympathies.

We ended up in neutral territory behind the black curtain
Which was when I popped the question,
"Hey, would you like to go see the band Heart at the Civic Center?"

She agreed and I picked her up at her apartment.
Heart was superb and we had a great time.
Then I dropped her off at home, said goodbye,
And never saw her or any show at the Baltimore Civic Center again.

Attman's of Lombard Street

Attman's Delicatessen located on Lombard Street
In the heart of Corned Beef Row was my late Sunday afternoon
Place to eat as a single man in my early twenties.

When I was knee-high in knishes and other Jewish delicacies,
I could be found sitting in the back seat with my brother and sister
As my dad drove the family down to Lombard Street.

We always frequented Jack's Corned beef back then
Because the sandwiches were premade
And there was plenty of family seating upstairs and down.
Then we walked over to Stone's Bakery
Where my dad would have his blood sugar raised at no extra charge.

But as soon as I had wheels and an appetite
With nothing to do on a Sunday afternoon,
My car was always pointed in the direction of Attman's.

They had fantastic corned beef and brisket to die for.
Plus, I knew the owner's son.
He lived across the street from my best friend on Northbrook
And whenever I came down, he'd always take care of me.

I would stand in line, grab a hard Keiser roll, hand it over the counter,
And have it stuffed with mouthwatering brisket.
Then, I made my way through the line joking with the guys,
And paid the mouthwatering blond cashier that stood by the door.

When the spirit moved me as it often did,
I would get a hot dog with fried bologna from her
Because the cash register was right in front of the grill.

Larry Levy

For some reason, the food always tasted better from her hands.
But my flirtation embellished with compliments got me nowhere.
She fixed me up with her younger sister but it wasn't the same.

There were no hurt feelings and we remained good friends
Which was important since I was down there once a week.

When I moved away from Chokeberry, I was always close enough
To bring home a lean corned beef with mustard on rye
For my dad waiting patiently at home.

Put it Back

I had been out of the house for several years
And on occasion would return to Wellwood
To catch up with my sister and the goings on at home.

Sometimes, I would park my car, sit in the driveway,
Where she and I would talk for hours
About life, liberty, and the pursuit of happiness in personal terms.

We had become good friends during her high school years
And even though she was seven years younger and a girl,
She was also genetically predisposed like her two brothers
To practical jokes, mischief, and mayhem.

One day when I drove down our street to see her and my dad --
After I had been out partying the night before --
I saw my sister walking the family dog sporting Hanes underwear.

Of course, the t-shirt and underpants were my dad's,
Lifted from his underwear drawer
As her way of reminding him that, "a dog *was* man's best friend."

Apparently, she also thought it was a good idea
For a dog to experience the usual human comforts
Not normally granted to those in the canine world.

After a lengthy walk where neighbors stared in disbelief,
And warned their kids of an upcoming revolution,
She undressed her good-natured obliging pet,
And returned my father's underwear to his dresser drawer.

My sister had learned what my brother and I
Failed to comprehend, despite my father's relentless efforts,
"If you borrow something, put it back where you found it."

Larry Levy

A Song to Remember

A neighbor of mine, two years my senior,
Had a sister about eight years older than me.
In 1965, she was the very definition of 'London Mod' –
Shoulder length hair with a flip, short dress, and go-go boots.

Her bedroom was downstairs in a two-level rancher
That took up much of the entire basement.

One day I found myself sitting in a chair facing her bed
While I waited for my friend to come rescue me.

After a few minutes, his sister came into the room,
Turned on the radio and sat on the edge of the bed.
Then this tall skinny guy who had sideburns and a goatee,
Sat down next to her and they started making out.

The Kinks, "All Day and All of the Night" came on the radio,
With those staggered power chords and suggestive lyrics.
I knew right then and there no school could ever teach me
What I learned that day simply by watching and listening.

Years later, on a Saturday night,
I wandered into a bar in Fell's Point,
And by chance saw her drinking and dancing with some friends.
After imagining every possible scenario of what could happen,
I approached her, re-introduced myself, and told her my story.

She left our amicable conversation flattered
While I felt saddened by the loss of innocence
And the reality that I could learn no more from her.

Still Well In Wellwood

But anytime I hear that song, that glorious song,
I am transported to the bedroom, the bed, the girl, the kiss,
And where the art of love began for me.

Epilogue

Larry Levy

The Shed

During high school two neighborhood buddies
Stopped by my house every morning on their way to Pikesville Sr.

After I gathered everything that I needed for the day, and when my,
"I-hate-everyone-that-walks-up-to-the-front-door" dog settled down,
The three of us walked up the street
And turned right into Chokeberry Court.

We sauntered to the very end of the court, went between two houses,
Walked through the backyard of the last house before Pikesville,
And stopped about fifty-feet from the line
That separated our neighborhood from the high school grounds.

There on the furthest point west
Before committing to another day of school,
Stood a little white utility shed
At the end of the yard where trees and shrubs yielded privacy.

The three of us took care of the business
Of pre-rolling a joint before the journey,
Then found a spot behind the shed that blocked the wind
And hid us from curious eyes peeking out of bedroom windows.

It was a paranoid reflex to hide activities where pot was concerned
Because on *our* side of the line, the owners of the shed were cool.
The father had a great sense of humor
And the mom was nice to all the kids.

The eldest daughter and I
Had known each other since elementary school
And she and her two sisters were part
Of what made the neighborhood great.
We were safer behind their shed than in our own backyards.

We finished our morning ritual in about ten minutes,
Yacked about what a drag certain teachers and classes were,
Then walked across the soccer and baseball field
And went into the side door at the top of Pikesville Sr.

II.

Several years after I graduated,
There were stories about other neighbors
That used the shed as the 'go-to' place to get high.

But looking back, 'The Shed' was more than just a stoner's rest stop.
It was the last holdout before crossing the line;
A line that physically and experientially
Separated one reality from another.

On one side was Wellwood; the happy-go-lucky place
Where good parents raised good kids
And where bad things rarely happened.
It was the 60's and a time of innocence when 'The Shed'
Was used for playing tag or storing bicycles.

But as we crossed over the line and moved a few years into the 70's,
A new reality took hold where yesterday's simple questions
Often turned into complex answers that most of us didn't want to hear.
Pot changed everything, so did sex, having a car, and divorce.

Most of us made it through intact,
Perhaps a little shaken, but not deterred.
Everyone had a story, a different perspective;

Their own 'Shed' as it were.
But one thing for certain, all was still well in Wellwood.

III.

The other day I was driving down Smith Ave from Seven Mile Lane,
A few blocks from Pikesville Senior High,
When "American Pie" by Don McLean came on the radio
Just like it did every day when I was eating lunch in the cafeteria.
It was surreal.

I tipped my hat to my alma mater as I drove past the school.
I decided to take a right on Lisburne Road
And replay the events that conspired with the music I now heard.

I stopped at the side of Wellwood where I used to play baseball,
Greek Dodge, and hang from the monkey bars on the playground.
For a moment, I was back in elementary school
When life was just beginning.

I continued, took a right onto Northbrook Road,
And when I came to the intersection of Northbrook and Labyrinth,
I pulled over to the right and stopped.

Across the street, two doors down on the left,
Was my best friend's house where I practically lived for many years.
I thought of all the times he and I played in his driveway
Or shot hoops in the back yard with his dad.

Then I turned right on Labyrinth and on the right-hand side
Recalled where another friend lived who owned a 10-speed bicycle;
An orange Schwinn *Varsity* that was the envy of me and my friends.

I pulled over and stopped at the corner of Labyrinth and Hatton.
The house across the street with the large bay windows
Faced me at an angle and appeared to be looking my way.

Still Well In Wellwood

I was reminded of a happy time back in the fifth grade
When I asked this pretty girl with blond hair to go steady.

On the opposite corner where she and I once held hands,
Was a house where a different kind of opportunity took place.
Looking to my right I was transported back to junior year
Where I almost had sex for the first time
With a friend of the girl who lived in the unsupervised home.
The distance between what once was and what didn't happen
Was fifty yards and six years apart.

As I made the turn from Labyrinth Road
And continued down Smith Avenue,
I went past Pikesville Sr. once more, this time a little teary-eyed.
Don Mclean was still singing about America's loss of innocence.

I turned my eyes to the left
Knowing 'The Shed' was no longer there.
I looked anyway hoping time would be kind to me
As I tried to recall the images of me and my friends:
How we looked, what we were wearing, and how we felt.

And then I came to.
I realized the events just relived were forty-seven years ago,
From a different time, and different place.
But in my mind and in my heart the reality was still the same.

I had one foot in and one foot out.

About the Author

Larry Levy is the author of two books of poetry, a book of humorous short stories, and an autobiography. His poetry has appeared in magazines, online, and in a poetry anthology. He has written the words and music for The Histrioniks, The Thromboes, and Muskrat Simms. As a multi-instrumentalist he has composed, engineered, and produced four albums under the pseudonym Instramentaclees and most recently a classical work for piano, guitar, and cello. His music has been played on MTV, Sirius XM, and on independent and college radio stations. He is a graduate of Towson University with a degree in Philosophy, and teaches drums to the rhythmically inquisitive. He lives in Baltimore with his wife and cat.

Other Books by the Author

Convoluted Whispers

The Catharsis of Form

Wait Awhile

When All Was Well in Wellwood

CPSIA information can be obtained
at www.ICGtesting.com
Printed in the USA
LVHW111353281021
701816LV00004B/162

9 781647 197803